How to Raise Highly Successful People

Learn How Successful People Lead!: How to Increase Your Influence & Raise a Boy

The ultimate guide to build a successful mind

Charles Bell

This Book is provided with the sole purpose of providing relevant information on a specific topic for which every reasonable effort has been made to ensure that it is both accurate and reasonable. Nevertheless, by purchasing this eBook, you consent to the fact that the author, as well as the publisher, are in no way experts on the topics contained herein, regardless of any claims as such that may be made within. As such, any suggestions or recommendations that are made within are done so purely for entertainment value. It is recommended that you always consult a professional prior to undertaking any of the advice or techniques discussed within.

This is a legally binding declaration that is considered both valid and fair by both the Committee of Publishers Association and the American Bar Association and should be considered as legally binding within the United States.

The reproduction, transmission, and duplication of any of the content found herein, including any specific or extended information, will be done as an illegal act regardless of the end form the information ultimately takes. This includes copied versions of the work, both physical, digital, and audio unless express consent of the Publisher is provided beforehand. Any additional rights reserved.

Furthermore, the information that can be found within the pages described forthwith shall be considered both accurate and truthful when it comes to the recounting of facts. As such, any use, correct or incorrect, of the provided information will render the Publisher free of responsibility as to the actions taken outside of their direct purview. Regardless, there are zero scenarios where the original author or the Publisher can be deemed liable in any fashion for any damages or hardships that may result from any of the information discussed herein.

Additionally, the information in the following pages is intended only for informational purposes and should thus be thought of as universal. As befitting its nature, it is presented without assurance regarding its prolonged validity or interim quality. Trademarks that are mentioned are done without written consent and can in no way be considered an endorsement from the trademark holder.

SYNOPSIS

THE ESTHER WOJCICKI STORY

One reason individuals go to Esther Wojcicki for parenting counsel is that her three girls are off-the-charts uber-successful: Susan is the CEO of YouTube, Janet is a professor at UC San Francisco, and Anne is the CEO of 23andMe.

In addition, Wojcicki has been an educator for a long time, helping fabricate globally reknowned media expressions program at Palo Alto High School. Products of the program include James Franco, the award-winning actor, director, and essayist; Jeremy Lin, a Harvard graduate and a member of the Atlanta Hawks; and Craig Vaughn, a developmental clinician with the Stanford Children's medical clinic.With her own kids, as well as others, Wojcicki has exhibited real success. So what's thesecret?

Her five-point direction comes as standards, not rules, which implies that not at all like much of the existing parenting guidance, it traverses the years, from giving birththroughtheir toddler's ages to how to respond when they grow up and fill the house. They are: trust, respect, independence, collaboration (cooperation), and kindness (TRICK). It comes down to cherishing your kids for what their identity is, not who you want them to be, and ditching the convention as much as you can. Children are more capable than parents may understand, and more in need of room to develop than their parents will give. Wojcicki follows an all around worn, yet still needed mantra of our time: let kids fail (the class test, the piano test, the tryout, the whatever).

"Kids are supposed to screw up as kids so they screw up less as adults," she notes, in her book, *'How to Raise Successful People'*stating that most instructors realize that failure is basic to learning, yet most parents appear in obscurity on this genuinely significant actuality.

The objective, she reminds us, is to make yourself unseen by bringing up kids to become effective, working people; upset constantly nor protected from failure. Confidence isn't conceived from over-protecting, it is conceived from doing and risking. Esther dressed her kids like they were adults from the beginning, confiding in them to get things done: to swim at year and a half; to separate in a supermarket; to go to the shop alone at three and four (she as of late did this with two granddaughters, dropping them off in Target and picking them up an hour later, and Susan was not amazed).

"You want your child to want to be with you, not to need to be with you," she writes further. Also, all the children do this: in the wake of galavanting around the globe, they all live near each other and eat together at least once per week.

She talks a great deal about trust: believing yourself to make the best choice and believing your child to do tasks when they know close to nothing or to make choices that are important to their age. Kids can do far more than parents give them acknowledgment for. Be that as it may, parents need to model the behavior they want to see, giving children consequences when they mess up, pardoning them for mistakes, and failing to bear resentment. Give a child a smartphone each time

the individual in question is upset, and that child won't learn stability, or how to overcome weariness.

"Children will hear you out—they want your endorsement and love—however on the off chance that they want to be upbeat, they will need to figure out how to hear themselves out," she says. "Use trust to get trust."

THE STORY

Wojcicki learned early not to trust anybody, or anything. At the point when her youngest sibling ate a container of aspirin at 16 months and four hospitals dismissed them, her mom, an Orthodox Jewish worker, didn't trust her impulses, took the hospital's statement, and David kicked the bucket. Her dad, also a worker, declared young men asnot needed for her, and was cold and far off. Wojcicki disposed of the rules of her childhood, got a grant to Berkley, met her husband (an experimental physicist), and afterward brought up three kids and assembled a classroom worked around with her senses, not what others told her enway the journey.

Her distrust of institutions and the standard way of thinking set her free. At the point when she began recollection 36 years back, counselor told her to construct a consistence based classroom, to "not smile until Christmas," and to punish kids to build up power. She, be that as it may, did the inverse: she trusted kids, giggled with them, and found a good pace. She gave them control over their learning as tasks and cooperation (way before it became stylish) and allowed them pick their passion and interests.

There were slips up, consequences, and, in the end, forgiveness. In any example, the school thought she was wild and incapable to "control" a classroom; at whatever point the chief visited, kids were talking and sometimes (gasp) having a great time. She let her kids in on the mystery: in the event that they weren't peaceful when the chief came in, she'd lose her cool. They then held it down.

Like all good parenting books, Wojcicki's tackles grit. Suffering difficulties is the thing that assembles grit, she notes. She refers to lamentable stories of kids who are panicked to fail in school for dread they will frustrate their parents; in the same way as other educators, Wojcicki has noticed an emotional trauma in kids who say they feel totally helpless. Be that as it may, she also observes the individuals who take a stab at something because they want it. "This is the thing that we want to bring out in our kids," she notes, "grit that streams from unbreakable and sharp drive and helps them through any example." (Along those lines, it very well may be instructed, she says). Kids need to pick their desires and passions: not parents. Anne was a capable artist, however she wanted to be an ice skater. So she became an ice skater.

And there you have it: **TRICK (Trust, Respect, Independence, Collaboration& Kindness).** This book applies Wojcicki's TRICK and many more parental strategies to create a framework for successful parenting. Chapter one outlines the important attribute of parents being sort of hands-off when dealing with their children's career choices (Independence); Chapter Two examines the place of friendship between the parent and children; should they be soulmate – will that not hurt the very soul of parenthood?This chapter echoes Trust and Respect. Chapter three discusses one of the hottest parenting topics: Discipline. What's the right way to discipline and not become an enemy to your child. This Chapter talks about Kindness as central theme. Finally Chapter Four touches on the issue of being a role model as a parent; this focuses on Collaboration. So the 4 components are well addressed.

CHAPTER ONE:

LET YOUR CHILD DISCOVER THEIR OWN PASSIONS

INDEPENDENCE

Growing up as a child yourself, you probably lived in an age where there was limited technology (at least comparative to now), and where "sensible' career options were largely limited to professions like medicine, law, engineering (hardware), economics and accounting and a few others. Back them-you may recall- parents will have their children do these courses or nothing else and anyone who is not in these fields is either a failure or nonentity. Today, people are into computer programming, software development, machine learning, ecommerce and digital marketing, music and filmography (full-time), and so on; careers that were either virtually non-existent back then or were looked down upon by our parents.

Similarly, in time past (those times that we grew up as children), career satisfaction or to put it properly, the ideal job, was one in which you could get the most financial rewards – in short, the highest paying careers were the best. But today, people put to consideration a wide range of factors which would have been considered negligible or outright silly back then. We hear things like work-life balance, propensity to create impact, alignment with passion, amongst others. In short, the high-paying job is not the more important job or career.

These are the times in which our children will grow, and as such we have to rethink how parents handle our children in relation to their passions (and career choices). Why so much hassle about career choices or passions or job selection? And why start this book with that?

We spend many hours every week, without end, doing work. Doing work you love makes life significantly more satisfying. Consequently, it's basic we work at directing and empowering our children in their mission to discover and accomplish work they love.

The status of work in contemporary social orders is the aftereffect of a long chronicled process. Work has become a focal sorting out component of both the judiciousness and the morals of our social orders. Relations of creation and use, production and consumption, are currently at the focal point of monetary association and sociallife. Notwithstanding its conspicuous conservative importance, work is also centralin a few different areas, in particular in its rolea a unifyingcomponent, as asource of social trades, and as an element of individual character. Work, at that point, can be seenas the mainstay of social organisation, however, to an enormous extent, as an importantpillar of theexistential association of individuals. It is preciselybecauseofthisthat work has become a crucial element in manymeasurements of social inclusion, such ashealth,housing, and relational networks.

How about we outline the significance of work both at the individual and the societal level:

For people, work is a significant element in structuring personal and social personality; family and social bonds; ways of making money, and thereby purchasing a number of essential and non-essential goods, services and utilities; daily routines; level of action; physical and mental well-being; self-confidence and self-esteem; a sense of self-esteem created by the feeling of contributing to society or the common good.

For societies, work is an important feature in: promoting community cohesion and wellbeing; increasing civic participation; reducing public spending in a range of welfare provisions (provided, of course, that work is performed in a decently paid job); promoting social and economic development; organizing social life at a macro level.

It is widely acknowledged, then, that work plays a positive role as a source of well-being and social mix. That is, work still has a fundamental role in the individual's psychological well-being and in structuring his/her biography, and thus in structuring the meaning he/she ascribes to his/her personal life. As an activity, work organises and provides meaning to the use of time in a society that has programmed its rhythms as a function of work. Work, then, is important in structuring daily life and in enabling a sense of continuity; also, it is an antidote against boredom and emptiness.

Given the above, informal, sometimes even illegal work, is sought not only because it gives financial gains to satisfy at least basic needs, but also because it helps organizes daily life and provides a sense of usefulness and occupation. Inversely, the loss of work is an important destabilizing factor, as revealed by the stories of marginalized individuals. Indeed, both ethnographic and biographic research show that unemployment, intermittent work, and poorly paying jobs play an important role in the social disqualification of street drug-users and homeless people. In a society that educates for work and keeps equating personal success not only with financial success but also with professional status, loss of work and the erosion of its quality have a strong negative impact on the ways individuals perceive themselves.

To sum up, work is a pillar in the building of societies. Indeed, the distinction between working and dangerous classes, between working individuals and lazy persons lies at the moral heart of our societies. Work has long become a frontier: it enables the distinction between normality and deviance. It has also become a disciplinary instrument, one that should enable directing individuals back to respect for norms and a sense of social usefulness. As such, it has also become a tool for regeneration (see, for example, the re-education of young offenders and the reintegration of former inmates).

While some theorists of post-industrial societies argued that work would gradually lose importance, namely through the transformations brought about by technological progress and the developing importance of leisure time, the truth is that the social and economic impact of the current surge of unemployment shows that work is still a central piece of our societies. Therefore, it is not only an indispensable means of enhancing individual senses of usefulness and belonging, but also of providing financial means.

Work has its good sides. Our life is an odd blend of various snapshots of activity and inaction, work and rest. Work gives us an internal inventive happiness. It spares us from the bluntness and weariness of life. It puts our energies to an appropriate use. Unused energies make issue in us. They make us truly unfortunate and intellectually troubled. Time balances substantial on our shoulders when there is no work. It gives us cash for our life hood. It makes our life significant and serene.

Laziness is more tedious and excruciating than work. Indeed, even the most unpaid, immaterial and upsetting work is superior to no work. For an extremely helpful and glad work, two things are essential. Valuable work is somewhat not so great in the starting, yet exceptionally lovely toward the end. For getting greatest delight from life, we should think about existence all in all, and how we contribute to it. Great Work pays and unfulfilling work devastates at the end. Each man who learns some helpful ability appreciates it till he develops himself totally. The component of helpfulness is a significant wellspring of bliss. At the point when a worker develops something new. He feels energized and raised and in this manner gets delight from his imaginative work.

Where there is no need, there would be no work. Where there is no work, there would be no happiness throughout everyday life.Ideally what would we be doing if there is no work?

Since careers are so important, then parents have to tread consciously when guiding their children as to how to go about it. Generally, I recommend that when mentoring their kids in the career selection process, parents have to be as "hands-off" as possible (I can imagine that slight frown on your forehead now). Yes this reeks Independence. But that is chiefly all there is to this. You might be saying, "but these kids are naïve, they know nothing; how much experience do they have?." Well I just feel you may be wrong. This is because resewresearch has shown that today's kids are smarter at younger ages than the past generation was at such ages. Why do you think we keep having new younger chess prodigies springing up every now and then? Why did we not have youngsters like Greta Thurnberg and Malala Yousafzai back then in the seventies and eighties.

These can be attributed to a number of factors:

Higher degrees of education

Children presently attend universities more than we as parents did and have high incredible early preparing programs before starting school. These two components, specifically, affect a child's latent capacity and achievement. There are huge modifications in school's curriculums.

Educational program these days doesn't focus on memorisation as it once did. Rather it centers around application to new conditions to solve problems. Research continually discloses to us that being a correct problem solver is fundamental to how appropriately we deal with situation and tasks.

Access to boundless resources

In contrast to a significant number of their parents and grandparents, kids today can now approach a worldwide universe of information by means of the online media and web. Think about this as a move from getting to an exceptionally little, neighborhood library to one that spans the length of the globe. What this significantly implies is that children don't have to just depend on their parents' thoughts or those of individuals in their neighborhood network to shape their reasoning.

They currently have access to a perpetual scope of books, pictures, information tables, recordings, web journals, games and different resources created by various individuals with various thoughts and information. Their worldwide library encourages them to think in manners children have always been unable to already.

They are better valued

Another good reason why children are surpassing our desires is on the grounds that we are letting them. It was once believed that children were unfilled vessels and we, as grown-ups, would fill them with our insight. Children were also expected to live by the standard that children ought to be seen and not heard. Both these lines of reasoning smother children's exercises and thinking. Children are probably not going to be successful people in a situation that works against their showing forth.

What every one of these variables mean for all intents and purpose is that they are sure changes to the way children are experiencing childhood. We don't have the foggiest idea how far our children can succeed; it's an energizing possibility. In any example, what we do know is the significance of having confidence in children and supporting them in their learning.

Better societal conciousness and responsibility

Due to better education and some other environmental factors, it can be generally agreed that our children are generally more inclined and interested in their societies and the socio-economic complexities that hold it together. That is why we have young chaps like Thurnberg and Yousafzai who are champions of climate action and girl-child education respectively. It is on record that there is an army of young intellectuals championing both conservative and liberal issues, a feat unfeasible years ago.

Furthermore research has shown that one of the most important things that children need out of their parents is the freedom to do things and figure out stuff on their own, and at inceadingly younger ages. A study by TP-LINK UK carried out in Britain suggested that children want substantial freedom from the time they clock eleven years. Such freedoms include access to the door key, freedom to stay online and do whatever they want on the internet for as long as possible, freedom to meet and go out with (new) friends, and many more. The study recommended - and we are reiterating that - that parents cannot stop this or oppose this with force of any kind. That will not be in your best interest. What you can do is to support this freedom but create frameworks to guide them so that this freedom only bears positives and not otherwise.

How you as a parent can support your child's Independence:

Start Early

In spite of the fact that children desire for boundary and limits, they likewise love and need to apply their independence. Starting when your child is a baby, regardless of whether they're just learning language abilities. You can let your child settle on choices like picking what type of cup they need to drink their juice from or which shirt they need to wear to childcare. Ordinary undertakings are also chances to support freedom. Let your child choose grain or eggs for breakfast, or pick the book to peruse for story time. She can assist you with picking the best apples in the market, or be accountable for discarding wrappers after play time on the play area. Letting your little youngster settle on choices and handle age-appropriate assignments cultivates his sprouting freedom, shows obligation, and can even form problem-comprehending abilities.

Keep as a main priority that more youthful children need more opportunity to execute their new dynamic aptitudes. Give yourself an additional ten minutes or so while permitting her to do things like dress herself or brush her own teeth. You'll progressively increasingly be well-suited to let her work on a portion of these independent abilities when you're not harried and feeling hurried in light of the fact that it's taking her an unfathomable length of time to choose which pair of tights to use for her hair,

Let Them Take Charge

As occupied guardians, we basically can't do everything. Nor should we need to! Particularly when we have children who can loan some assistance.

One of the most tedious jobs in our family unit is providing suppers. I'll concede, I very much want preparing a pleasant supper for family than washing a heap of messy whites, however making nourishment for eight hungry mouths three times each day is tedious. You can let your children gain proficiency with their way around the pantry; they should have early acquaintances with the kitchen. More youthful children can help set and gather the dishes while more older children can get familiar with the delights of preparing a plate of mixed greens (here and there truly!), assisting with arranging menus, and going along to do shopping for food.

Create space for Ample Unstructured Time

Another approach to assist your child in increasing some freedom is to permit him to have pockets of personal time. This may appear as though a senseless and unproductive approach to enable your child to win his wings, however many specialists would oppose this idea.

Children need to figure out how to discover things that fascinate them and to have the chance to invest energy in the things they like. Guardians can urge children to be progressively autonomous by not overscheduling all their extra time after school and on the weekends. Rather, offer up a personal time where he can check out his own interests. Discover approaches to sustain his imagination without steady direction on the best way to remain occupied.

Don't Bail Them Out

As guardians, we need to protect our children from trouble's path and from encountering life's damages and frustrations. In addition to the fact that that is outlandish, it's not beneficial. Give your child the endowment of permitting him to learn from his mistakes.

In Psychology Today's article, *Mistakes Improve Children's Learning*, Marilyn Price-Mitchell, Ph.D., composes that society constrains children's ability to be great. Thus, guardians feed into this by concealing their children's mistakes. That even incorporates things like remedying school assignments to help improve their scores! Mitchell prescribes that guardians abstain from saving children from their mistakes. Rather, she proposes helping them center around finding an answer. She also says that children ought to be urged to take obligation regarding their mistakes as opposed to accusing others.

By not rescuing your child when he does something incorrectly, you offer him a major advance in achieving more freedom. You instruct him that he has to own up to his bad behavior. For instance, take the story of a high school kid who lost his chemistry course book. He decided to go to the neighborhood frozen yogurt shop after end of the year tests and, rather than placing the book in his storage or his knapsack, he left it on a table in the cafeteria. The reason? He would not like to take an opportunity to take care of it. At that point, as opposed to coming back to the cafeteria after the frozen yogurt hurry to get the book, he took off to play ball. He figured he could get the book in the early next day..

At the point when he returned the next day, the book was no more. He looked all over, yet without much of any result. At the point when it came time to turn in the book, he went to his mother and confessed that he was unable to find it. The school's approach is "no book, no final grade." The expense of the book is $80. At the point when he at last admitted to her what had occurred, she commended him for conceding his mistake yet disclosed to him he would need to make sense of how to pay for it all alone. He'll pay for the book out of his first summer check or he'll need to retake Chemistry next year.

Let them pay their way

When your kids start learning a skill or working side jobs, you can start showing them how to set aside and spending plan their cash. On the off chance that your kids find out about money management while they're youthful, they'll have a decent possibility of getting monetarily dependable as grown-ups. Learning money management unquestionably cultivates a basic, deep rooted foundation of your child's autonomy.

Show Self-Help

In Psychology Today's *Teaching Your Adolescent Independence*, Carl E Pickhardt, Ph.D., composes that there are in any event four segments guardians can utilize when teaching independence:

- Responsibility
- Accountability
- Work
- Self-help

All standing for RAWS.

Self-help can be a problem at times since we as guardians are so eager to get the show on the road to hop in and take care of our child's problems for them. Dr. Pickhardt's recommendation is to refrain from helping your child, so she gets an opportunity to develop answers all alone. This may mean enduring it when your 3-year old girl can't get her coat unzipped in light of the fact that she despite everything has her gloves on. Allow her two or three minutes to perceive how she handles the problem all alone.

Turn over the reins

Each and every day is loaded up with many decisions. Apple or banana? Nutty spread or ham and cheddar? Red shoes or blue?

Permitting your children to settle on those little decisions gives them a feeling of control and domain over their lives which prompts autonomous reasoning. It likewise helps them take responsibility for decisions – for reasons unknown that nutty spread sandwich tastes so much better since they picked it!

Encourage problem solving

Control your craving to bounce in and fix. At the point when a problem emerges, pause. Offer your child the chance to think of fixes themselves.

Ask them "How?" questions. "How might you cause your sister to feel better after you took her doll and broke it?" "How might you ensure you find solution to this maths problem?" if you need them to have an independent mind, don't provide all the appropriate responses.

Encouraging family contributions

Each individual member of the family assumes an important job in an effectively running family unit. From setting out napkins to getting toys – urging kids to contribute in age-appropriate ways instructs them that they are a piece of an important group that needs them! This fabricates their certainty and urges them to need to do much more.

Promote effort

That perfectionist pang? It's exaggerated and it causes a LOT of tension for kids. Truth be told, a few kids are so secured in the dread of disappointment – they won't attempt. They rather don't dare attempt anything because of the fear of mistakes and the attendant disapproval that arises therefrom.

Urge your kids to attempt new things, to leave their usual ranges of familiarity and be imaginative without the strain to succeed or win or be great. At the point when you do, they'll be all the more ready to take on new assignments in future.

When kids tend to be independent and freedom-minded from such young ages, it will easy for them to choose careers that fit their skills. This has been confirmed by experts. Julie Lythcott-Haims, former Dean of Freshmen at Stanford University, noted in a TED Talk that one of the traits common to successful children is that they have parents who let them be independent.

A Note of Caution

Now, even though independence is just so important, we have to note that we are not just recommending a "sit-down-and-watch-how-things-go" approach. You are their *guardian*. And as such, you should still be involved in their career choice and development. So how do you get involved in the process of their career choice-making without becoming unnecessarily over-indulgent and still leaving room for enough independence? The tips below should help.

Oppose regarding your child as an extension of you

Your child is a special person. They are not you. The things that may make you totally angry about a specific job may be the things they completely love doing. Fight the temptation to advise your child to maintain a strategic distance from a specific way since it's something that doesn't fascinate you. Your child probably won't be keen on going to the university you attended or doing the work you do.

Help your child discover their strengths and passions

Urge your child to visit with a career instructor to take inclination tests. The Myers-Briggs test, Strong Inventory, and Holland Code were three of the tests that have been adjudged very good. While I don't prescribe basing enormous choices off of one test, I do trust it's exceptionally gainful to take an assortment of evaluations and search for patterns among the outcomes. In the event that your child is keen on a profession that doesn't seem to agree with their normal strengths, that doesn't mean you have to promptly cancel out that choice. Rather, conceptualize how your child could carry their natural strengths to that field. Their exceptional point of view and strengths in that field could permit them to make an extremely interesting, important commitment.

Have them take the strengths evaluation in the book *Strengths Finder 2.0* by Tom Rath. Pay regard for what comes easily to them that others appear to battle with. Having an extraordinary comprehension of their inborn strengths will empower you to help them augment these strengths. Likewise, help them make sense of what fascinates them.

Help find a mentor for your child

Look for a positive, empowering good example for your child. In the event that your child shows solid enthusiasm for a specific profession, help your child locate a worthy mentor in that field. Having an incredible mentor can fuel your child's career goals.

Expose your child to an assortment of exercises to perceive what arouses their curiosity

Give your child chances to attempt new exercises. Expose them to nature, human expressions, science, historical centers, creatures, travel, individuals… there are such huge numbers of chances to partake in tasks together. Pay consideration regarding what arouses their curiosity. In the event that there is a subject they are interested about or they show energy towards, urge them to concentrateon that point. As a rule, the choice to pick a specific profession comes bit by bit, as individuals keep on investigating their inclinations as time passes by.

Discover your tribe, and urge your child to discover theirs

As Jim Rohn stated, "You are the average of the 5 individuals you spend time withwith." As a parent, have you assembled a magnificent tribe of individuals around you? Also, would you say you are urging your child to discover their tribe? Challenge your child to escape their customary range of familiarity and get involved with others outside their zone. Regardless of whether it's games, an association, a business club, or any of the many different prospects, urge your child to spend time with motivating friends. Who your child decides to spend time with can enormously influence how big they dream, what they accept is conceivable, and the open doors they look for. Having a stunning tribe of individuals throughout their life will help them develop into their maximum capacity and can influence many choices they make.

Set a good model

Your child keeps a close eye on you, so work on being an extraordinary example of doing work you appreciate. At the point when your child sees you building a career you truly love, they will realize that it's feasible for them to likewise discover and accomplish work they love. You're never too old to even consider spending additional time doing what you love, so look for what illuminates you and accomplish a greater amount of what you love and less of the unimportant garbage.

Be persistent and encouraging

Remind your child that the journey to accomplish work they loves is regularly a long process of self-discovery and testing. They may change course as they explore their career way. Show love toward your child during these troublesome choices, and urge them to continue learning progressively about themselves so they can continue developing into the astounding individual they are intended to be.

Have a conversation with your child about their inclinations.

Ask your child what their preferred subject is in school. Examine your child's leisure activities and extracurricular exercises. Make note of what they suck at just as what they appreciate. Tune in and be aware of things that your child shows enthusiasm for during this conversation.

You may start the conversation by saying something like "So what is your preferred class this year?" For instance, they may appreciate math and football, however just be acceptable at math.

Use career assessment devices to help pinpoint your child's strengths.

Your child is still yet developing and forming into aadultand might be amazed to discover that they have explicit strengths that could be valuable in a profession. Instruments, for example, character assessments and state sanctioned tests, for example, the SAT or ASVAB are intended to pinpoint a child's strengths. Understanding their strengths will permit them to start taking an interest in professions that will permit them to utilize their novel gifts.

For instance, a few children truly have a skill for technology. If so, a career in an IT field may be an incredible fit.

Research distinctive career options with your child.

Utilize the abilities and interests that you related to your child to direct your search. Incorporate things like compensation, benefits, and run of the mill work plan for every profession you examine. You can discover information about various career fields on the web, at career fairs, and by counseling professionals and organizations in that field.

However, look past traditional careers. Regular careers, for example, teachers, specialists, and legal advisors are talked about every now and then. Many children will have no enthusiasm for these fields, and ought to be exposed to fresher fields. Science and technology fields are changing each day, just like human expressions. Be available to taking a look at nontraditional careers just as the traditional careers.

For instance, the web has offered a tremendous oppourtunity for bloggers. This profession didn't exist a hundred years prior, yet it is presently a suitable method to bring home the money.

Converse with individuals who work in fields important to your child.

You can discover professionals in practically any field in the phonebook or on the web. Get in touch with them and check whether they would meet with your child. A direct meeting is frequently more telling than the exploration insights you find on the web. Have your child demand a gathering with them and set out a rundown of inquiries to pose to them. A few models may be:

What does their everyday work plan look like?

What kind of education or preparing did they have to meet all requirements for this position?

What is the run of the mill pay for this profession?

Do they enjoy most of their work?.

Urge your child to pick up practical experience in their field.

Networking and experience are similarly as important as education and preparing. There are a few different ways to pick up understanding and contacts in a specific field including chipping in, shadowing, and internships. Disclose to your child ethat the more administration they take, paid or unpaid, the more genuinely they will be taken later on by managers.

Children should start fabricating their resume as early as soon as possible.

CHAPTER TWO:

BUILD ROCK SOLID RELATIONSHIPS

TRUST

One big problem that children have with their children and which is a major causative factor of most of the teenage and childhood deliquencies that we have is the lack of good relationship and rapport between parents and their children. To develop children that are all-rounded and prepared for success, parents have to become their life partners. They have to hold them hand-in-hand throughout the different phases of their lives; so much vices exist out there- drugs, bullying, and children can easily fall prey to these undesirable habits which can derail them from their passions and future. Most of these vices are actually not learnt within the home or family but picked up outside from friends through the instrumentality of what is known as peer pressure. And you know what, this relating with friends cannot be prevented because parents will not always be with their children; and we cannot prevent them from going to places where they will mingle with other kids; they will relate with others in the neighborhood, they will go to schools (and eventually, college). So the interaction can never be prevented.

What the parents can do is to make the negative traits be impressed upon them not to become a part of them. This can be done effectively by being friends of their kids.

However a note of caution: there are many arguments against parents being close friends with their kids. In fact some of these are advanced by experts.

In their book, *The Narcissism Epidemic*, writers Jean Twenge and W. Keith Campbell note that guardians add to the problem when they attempt to become a close acquaintance with their kids. That is on the grounds that guardians who style themselves as "pals" may think that it is difficult to implement rules and principles.

Different researchers point to the disadvantages of regarding children as friends. Kids may get worried by adverse personal closeness. For instance, when researchers met the pre-adult little young girls in a school, they found that young ladies were bound to encounter mental pain if their mothers made nitty gritty exposures to them about their spending habits, businesses, personal problems, and pessimistic emotions about their exes.

To certain individuals, friendship signifies "no one is in charge." Friendship is carefully libertarian. Neither one of the partners practices authority over the other. On the off chance that this is the thing that you mean by "friendship," at that point the inquiry is by all accounts about the impacts of tolerant (or even careless) child rearing.

Research proposes that kids improve when their parents show love and authorize age-appropriate cutoff points on their children's conduct. There is also proof that tolerant child rearing meddles with the advancement of self-control. For instance, an investigation of African-

American children solicited kids to consider an arrangement from theoretical circumstances that included frustration and struggle. The kids who portrayed their parents as progressively tolerant were also bound to state that they would react fiercely to circumstances of contention.

Friendship may likewise cause problems on the off chance that it signifies regarding a child as aadultadvisor.actually, it's not by any means obvious that cozy confessions from guardians cause kids to feel like companions - at any rate not when the confessions are upsetting. In the examination referenced above, increasingly point by point revelations from mothers were not connected with more prominent sentiments of closeness in their little girls.

Yet, not every single personal confession are of a troubling sort, and all things considered, a few types of sharing fortify the parent-child relationship. In an investigation of 790 Dutch young people, researchers found that kids who announced offering insider facts to their parents had better connections and lower paces of deliquency. Another investigation of Swedish children found that the way to great conduct and family amicability wasn't awkward parental reconnaissance. It was the child's discernment that his parents confided in him.

So closeness needn't infer that you are troubling your child with your personal difficulties. Also, conveying trust needn't send the message that "anything goes."

Guardians can construct close, personal associations with their kids and still stay capable grown-ups. Few out of every odd friendship depends on sharing equivalent status.

Friendships with power figures: Warmth, trust, companionship...and limits Consider the parent who authorizes confines and abstains from stressing her kids with point by point records of her adultpersonal problems. She is above all else a mother to her kids. Be that as it may, she may likewise consider herself to be a companion since she and her kids share a feeling of common faithfulness, trust, and regard.

Also... She regards her children as people with minds of their own. She chats with her kids about their considerations, expectations, thoughts, and sentiments. She shares bits of her own "psychological life" with them- - not the bits liable to trouble kids, yet bits that help kids consider themselves as people (Example: "I'm troubled. I wish we could go to Disneyland, as well, yet we can't manage the cost of it.")

This thought of friendship appears to be in sync with the research verdict on secure connections, "mind-minded child rearing," inductive order (disclosing why it's important to adhere to rules), and legitimate child rearing (child rearing that is warm and responsive, yet in addition related with exclusive expectations).

Is this truly friendship?

It is anything but a carefully libertarian friendship. It's increasingly similar to the kind of friendship that a few grown-ups manage to have with power figures- - like senior partners, directors, mentors, network pioneers, or strict counselors. The two parties regard one another. They care about and trust one another. They can have important discussions and appreciate each other's conversation in casual settings. Be that as it may, there are superiors. The prevailing party needs to remain quiet about some information. Also, there are times when the prevailing party must exercise his position.

Is it justified, despite all the trouble? I guess it relies upon your personal attributes and social convictions. Also, perhaps a few kids don't adjust well to the parent-as-definitive companion model.Be that as it may, this pertains a lot Western kids who are thought as usually receptive of the reasonable, friendly,authoritative approach to child rearing.

Mind-minded child rearing" seems to add to a child's advancement of compassion. For example:

- Inductive order (clarifying the purposes behind principles and the social, moral outcomes of terrible conduct) is connected with increasing self-control, not so much hostility, but rather with more developed moral thinking.

- Friendly, objective, responsive guardians may have progressively moral impact over their young people. In one examination, American understudies were given speculative good choices and asked how they would handle them. Understudies raised by friendly guardians were more probable than the other kids to reference their parents - not their friends – as to who was responsible for their good judgement.

- Close parent-child connections based on trust and open communication may protect youths from risky conduct. In an investigation of American ninth and tenth graders, researchers discovered children were bound to take part in sexual action in the event that they were alone. Be that as it may, friendly parent-child connections were important, as well. Young ladies who saw their parents as trusting were less inclined to take part in sexual promiscuity, tobacco, and cannabis use. Young men who saw their parents as all the more trusting were more averse to use alcohol.

From the above it is evidenced that a one-cap-fits-all approach does not make full sense. Hence a mixture of strategy. We are not recommending a system where you become their friends to the extent that no one knows the parent or who is in charge anymore. There is a need for a balance. You have to create that close and friendly relationship with your children, at the same time you have to be discretionary about it.

Building trust with your child is important. It is the significant structure square to any relationship. This really promotes collaboration and lessens disobedience.

The minute a child is conceived, the obligation of confidence starts developing. Be that as it may, as guardians, we can't simply concludeand state, "My child trusts me." Our activities and words consistently need to match to clarify the genuine and fair significance of being trustworthy. A seed of uncertainty can develop into a major tree of low self-regard in a child.

An absence of trust in a parent-child relationship is showed through different practices. Regardless of whether it is stealing money, escaping around evening time, punching openings through dividers, or not keeping promises, it is each a sign that the degree of trust in your relationship with your child can be improved.

Trust, obviously, is a 2-way street and it's hard for one individual to trust another if the other individual isn't behaviourally or verbally dependable. While your teenager may trust that you will provide nourishment, a home, and garments the story doesn't end there. Children likewise need to trust that parents will be there and respond empathetically when they commit an error, they need the parents to invest quality time with them and not ignore them for work or other duties, they need parents to get some information about what is happening throughout their everyday life and be really interested, they need parents to keep their assertion, they have to have family suppers together regularly where positive talk takes spot and great stories are exchanged, they need parents to provide a sheltered home without consistent antagonistic vibe or contentions, and they need parents to teach right conduct. Every one of these things exhibit care and thus fabricate trust.

Ordinarily, when children don't get satisfactory consideration from one or the two guardians, they confuse the conduct as an absence of care. So as to recover a portion of that consideration they will at that point take part in flawed conduct that regularly inspires a reaction from mother or father (or both). All things considered, any sort of consideration can be superior to no consideration. ***So how can you build that close relationship with children?***

These tips should be helpful:

- **Straight talk**

    Being straightforward is the most important component in building trust. Manipulative words and activities place question in the child's mind and will in the end shield them from trusting you. Children are shrewd in checking good and bad. So don't attempt to shield reality. One way you can do this, while as yet clutching a adultlevel mystery is to just recognize that there is some problem that needs to be addressed and since you love the child and don't need him/her to be pestered by it, you can't divulge the information. It's only an example, however you get the idea there. You don't need to simply forget about them… you basically need to clarify it in anbrilliant way. Moreover guarantee him/her that soon you will sift through everything and afterward nobody should stress.

    Lesson: Self-confidence and personal regard are then alsobuilt up in the child.\

- **Stay true to your commitment**

    Another important lesson towards building trust is to be committed. Guardians go about as a good example for their children so some of the time when we flounder, children vacillate.

    Kids have an intrinsic craft of perusing the non-verbal communication of individuals around them. They rapidly get feelings and promptly sense what we are thinking. So when you make a commitment, attempt your best to satisfy it. In the event that in any way, shape or form, you can't stay faithful to your commitment, at that point provide a legitimate reason rather than complaints. Recognize that you couldn't satisfy the promise, yet don't accuse others. That sets an inappropriate model.

Ordinarily the both parents and children will make promises and afterward drop because of absence of time, misconduct, other all the more engaging social exercises, and so forth. This is the common approach to decrease trust in one another. Similarly as children need to stay faithful to their commitments to their parents, guardians need to stay faithful to their obligations to their children.

Lesson: Parents can now and then commit errors too since we are for the most part humans. The important thing is to learn from the mistakes.

- **Communicate however consistently Make the first move**

At the point when re-building trust, it is generally the job of the parent to make the first move. A few guardians trust that youngsters will make the initial move, thinking their children need to show they are keen on change. As a parent you have to set the model first. At the point when uncertain of how to manage the circumstance, youngsters may carry on such that it will exacerbate the problem.

Communication is the foundation of trust. The more you talk straightforwardly with your child, the more your relationship will develop. Search out occasions to talk with your child. Ask about their assessment on something. Listen with love, sympathy, and without judgment.

Communication is an important advance to many things and this incorporates building trust. It is hard to improve your trust in the event that you are not imparting your points of view and what is happening in one another's lives.

- **Listen first**

A considerable amount of us sadly hear our children, however not so much listening to them. The first step is to turn on your "listening" mode. In the process, comprehend what the child is letting you know. Try not to guess things. Likewise, go above and beyond to comprehend the sentiments of the child before turning out with any solution or passing a judgment. Comprehend and attempt to decide whether the child truly is stressed or is simply just being anxious. Usually the child simply needs you to listen, maybe to just understand things in a specific request in his/her mind. So listen as opposed to guessing.

Trust starts in earliest stages of the child's development. At the point when a child is sad, they have to realize that their parent will react to them in a positive way. Smile and delicately talk to your child as you attempt to perceive what they're trying to pass across. Is it accurate to say that he is eager, stressed, tired, or just plain anxious? Maybe he's exhausted or needs some reassuring? Reacting to your baby's needs is the first means to building trust.

Lesson: Children figure out how to all the more likely distinguish their feelings and build up a problem-solving disposition.

- **Show respect**

Give earnest consideration and grace while the child talks. Let the child feel respected by making him feel he is important. The child has to realize that he/she is important. None of us trust an individual who doesn't show respect. Since a child is youthful and seemingly innocent to us, we will in general overlook that these little blessed kidsalso have feelings and a feeling of poise. Using defamatory comments or not respecting their considerations gives them enough reason not to trust.

Treating one another and addressing one another (and about one another) with respect is important to building trust. It is hard to build up a trusting relationship as a child if you're addressed disrespectfully or on the off chance that you catch your parent (or your child) castigating you.

Lesson: A child's self-esteem gets supported. Also the child figures out how to respect others.

- **Engender transparency and practice accountability**

Continuously make sure to give goodinformation and take charge of your activities. On the off chance that understanding everything is hard for the child, at that point recognize that you can't share all the taks as it may be too hard to even think about understanding.

Guarantee them that you are doing whatever it takes not to conceal something, however are protecting them from getting injured (emotionally). The more you wind the information, the more disarray wins and henceforth mistrust is fostered.

Lesson: Your child figures out how to communicate sincerely and clearly.

- **Process and patience**

As you wouldn't anticipate that your child should get a handle on some other "grown-up" idea quickly, you will need to exercise a whole lot of patience and perseverance and be ready to see through the process. In any case, that is really something to be happy for. The time we take in the trust-building process isn't time that is squandered. Rather, consistently turns into a day loaded up with quality connection and authentic, fair discussion with your young one. Treasure and savor these days and this time together, and understand that you are really fabricating genuinely splendid attributes in them. Indeed, this takes time... but since it takes time implies that they won't be qualities that can be effectively torn down.

Building a trusting relationship occurs after some time. Now and again you may feel like your relationship is progressing and at different occasions you may feel it is crumbling. During these occasions, it is important you keep your positive and confident attitude and proceed with your arrangement of building a trusting relationship. Your effort extra time will bring great outcomes.

For a trusting relationship to be created there must be consistency (or unwavering persistence) in the relationship. The more frequently every one of you shows that you can be trusted, the more probable you will be trusted. Consistency fortifies each relationship.

- **Acknowledging and Appreciating Honesty**

Appreciating honesty is a vital component of building a trusting relationship with your child. Make it understood to your children that you value it when they are straightforward. This will fabricate an extremely trusting connection among you and your child. Beside that, you will help your child in turning into an individual of integrity. As the idiom goes - say what you mean and mean what you say.

- **Avoid making promises**

Try not to make promises to your children in the that you can't keep them. This can be a significant test as circumstances may change. However, attempt to fulfill them as breaking promises could be wrecking to your relationship with your child. In the event that you state you are going to watch a soccer match in the end of the week, ensure you will do only that supposing that you don't, the next time you promise something, they will question if you are extremely genuine about it. On the off chance that it appears that you probably won't have the option to stay faithful to your commitment, tell your child ahead of time and clarify why.

RESPECT

This must be mutual. That is, reciprocal, the children must respect and the parent must in turn do the same. Respect matters. It is a basic idea for children to comprehend and follow up on. The first spot they start to find out about respect is in the home. They are relied upon to demonstrate respect to their parents early on, yet the most ideal way they figure out how is through their parents.

Parents should respect their child since that is the manner by which the child will figure out how to respect themselves. Parents fill in as the first and most important good example for everything a child does now and further down the road. The relationship a child has with their parents profoundly affects the child's advancement. Parents have the ability to teach their kids the best way to respect others and themselves. Parents who purposefully model appropriate conduct day by day for their kids are bound to encourage the advancement of balanced youthful grown-ups who know how and why they should treat others well.

You might be surprised but respecting your child as a human rather than just merely a child endears that child to you.

There are many reasons why parents should respect their children. They include:

It creates better connection

Children figure out how to respond to circumstances from everyone around them. There is nobody they learn more from than their parents.

We program them, and they figure out how to respond dependent on the information and training they get from us. Each time they spill something, break something, accomplish something out of request, or miss a detail and get criticism from us they disguise what they are told about the occasion.

Each occurrence is a chance to give grace and love to a child who probably didn't intend to do anything incorrectly. The idea of the reaction they get has a high probability of turning into the manner in which they rate themselves. You are programming their inward voice.

It is actually something difficult to do. Some of the time you simply need to escape the house and are attempting to move them along. Different occasions, you have just rehashed yourself multiple occasions and are becoming upset.

These are minutes where self-restraint and balance will work well for you. At the point when you think back, you will see these were chances to buildclose association with them. On the off chance that you teach your child to love themselves they will be bound to feel associated with you, and you will end up being a model for patience and generosity.

On the off chance that you are hard on them all the time they will figure out how to be hard on themselves as well, and they will always recollect where they discovered that too.

In the two situations, the child will figure out how to tidy up the spilled milk. Be that as it may, just in one will they learn patience, elegance, and benevolence in the process.

Creates positive self image of yourself

Individuals recollect how you affected them before they recall what you said or did at a particular point. There is no spot where this is more genuine than with our own children. Kids recall their passionate reactions to occasions first. Their brains are not prepared to thoroughly think about everything around them. Many negative encounters make negative impressions.

On the off chance that your child builds up a negative impression of you after some time they will be less inclined to need to follow your model, which might be hinder the building of a rock-solid relationship with them. Your capacity to make your child a willing pupil relies upon a positive relationship with your child.

That doesn't mean you need to be too gentle. The human brains doesn't completely form until age about 25. They won't be equipped for complete adultlevel thinking until that time. On the off chance that you get this, at that point you comprehend that how you cause your kids to feel is a colossal factor in whether they will eventually turn out well.

However, in the event that they feel associated with you enough to trust you, at that point they will be bound to tail you until they make sense of respect for themselves. As they experience this process, they will ideally be admiring you all the time.

Creates Positive Self-Image

The individual a child looks up to (or doesn't) will assume a huge role in shaping the way they see themselves. Kids who are instructed to show respect and have it demonstrated for them in the home grow great relationship propensities and figure out how to approach others with respect.

The individuals who don't, battle to figure out how to treat others. As they go down either way, they start to disguise the lessons of their day by day activities. Try not to believe it's everything about the big occasions. Little day by day events can dramatically affect how a child sees themselves. As a child and young person, observation is molded significantly more by feeling than by rationale or logic.

Shapes their interaction with others

Customarily, how grown-ups treat others is an impression of how they treat themselves. Encouraging your child to be thoughtful to themselves is a major advance you can take to cultivate in them a capacity to have solid associations with others.

Every day they will take a little advance forward on their way to self-awareness. You pick whether you need that way to be cleared with a positive self-view or a negative self-view. As they experience life they will figure out what they organize because of what they have realized through their encounters especially those with you.

On the off chance that they have been educated to show respect, consideration, and compassion to themselves as well as other people as a child they will be bound to do as such as a grown-up.

In the event that their inward compass is so centered around not destroying things since they need to hit the nail on the head the first occasion when they will overlook the human component that goes into the entirety of our every day encounters and will do things and make decisions over individuals and connections. They won't realize that individuals matter more in life than assignments.

Earns them even further respect from others

You show your child social competence consistently. The propensities your child procures in your house is the thing that they will take out into the world.

This includes respect. The best method to guarantee they figure out how to respect others is to show how it ought to be done in your own home. As you do, they will learn from their encounters with you much more than they ever could learn by being told or by reading it in a book. The effect of this methodology can be seen from the two sides. Take a minute to consider a day with the family where things simply weren't working out positively. We as a whole have them.

Did you shout at your child? Provided that this is true, how could they respond? Is it accurate to say that they were disturbed? Did you see them start to treat others the manner in which they had been dealt with? Do they have a kin that they started shouting at along these lines to what they had recently experienced?

So in practical terms, how can you show or prove respect in your children without handing the baton of control to them?

Permit your child to make choices about their body.

Similarly as we would not attack a grown-ups physical space, nor should we do as such with a child. Permit your child to choose whether or not to embrace somebody; don't compel her or make her vibe blameworthy in the event that she doesn't want to hug afrriend at that point. The message you send your child when you permit him to make choices about his body currently can affect how he feels about his privileges and capacity in future.

One way that we can respect our children and show them the respect they deserve is to give them choices or permit them to make choices. For instance, we shouldn't spread out everything the child's going to wear the next day at school if the child has positively no decision in the issue. By asking children, "What might you want to wear at school tomorrow," you show them you value their assessment and what they believe is important to them. Obviously this doesn't mean we're to let them wear things that are not appropriate, however it's a respectable thing to permit your child some contribution to their ownlife

Use good manners while connecting with children.

This may sound senseless, yet it makes sense! At the point when we model care and politeness, we are not just showing them the proper method to treat all individuals (big and small), we are likewise imparting in them a feeling of self-respect.

React to mistakes with grace

This implies ceasing from snickering when your child makes a mistake, or tumbles down, or gets into his jeans in reverse, or stalls out in his hair. It might be amusing to us, yet to a child, it very well may be mortifying to be giggled at when he makes a mistake.

Letting them do things themselves

We regularly serve children; and this isn't just a demonstration of servility toward them, however it is risky, since it will in general choke out their useful unconstrained movement. Instead of serving your child and hopping in continually to help, first attempt to accept that your child can do it without anyone else. Permitting your child to pour her own milk, to tidy up after himself, to get herself dressed, to carry his own bowl of soup to the table for lunch, will enable your child, support his confidence, and increase his capacity to do that specific assignment; all things considered, learning is doing.

Listen

Permit your child to speak for herself, regardless of whether it has an inclination that it's requiring some investment to get it hard and fast. Use patience and eye to eye connection, and abstain from hindering or completing her sentences. At the point when you show your child that what she needs to state matters, you demonstrate her to use her voice in a wide range of circumstances.

Allowing them their privacy

Some portion of showing respect to children is recollecting that a few things can be humiliating for them, and that they rely on you to keep their private lives... private. For example, avoid talking about your child to fellow adults before your child. Showing respect includes monitoring your child's genuine emotions, and doing so will cement the trust you, and will keep on developing with time, given that you are straightforward and solid.

Hesitate to Respond

In the event that you in some cases feel like you're on the receiving end of your child's flood of inquiries, remain connected with them, show interest, however don't rush to offer a response.

At the point when parents react rapidly to each address, solicitation, or request, children figure out how to rely upon quick reactions and feel disappointed when parents don't react with speed. Whenever we don't offer a child a chance to make sense of the response for himself, we show an absence of confidence in his capacities and sow the seeds of helplessness and over-reliance on the parents.

To abstain from encouraging helplessness, I urge parents to react with calm. This is an awesome method to put the monkey on your child's back and offer him the chance to grapple with the current circumstance.

Use kind and firm discipline to instruct, not to punish.

Discipline intends to instruct or to prepare, not to punish. It doesn't need to be punitive. Actually, research have shown that positive discipline is much more successful and longer-enduring than punitive systems.

On the off chance that we discipline with a threatening or harsh tone when our kids have done something incorrectly, we are showing them how to be pitiless and brutal to other individuals who make mistakes. Who doesn't make mistakes?

Suppose you make a senseless mistake at work and the supervisor talks down to you in a belittling manner. That must feel extremely humiliating, isn't that so? Would any of us, along these lines, have more respect for this boss? No, right? The same with children, being cruel or utilizing defamatory discipline won't win us respect.

In any case, positive discipline isn't equivalent to being "soft" or lenient. One can be firm and kind simultaneously while training.

Defining firm limits and adhering to them are the keys to effective discipline.

Make amends when you make mistakes

A mature, respectful adult acknowledges responsibility and apologizes when the individual in question makes mistakes.

Saying 'sorry' to your child doesn't undermine your position as a parent. In actuality, you are fortifying your position and validity. You are exhibiting trustworthiness and building trust with your child.

Be a model of honesty to our child

regardless of whether it's humiliating now and again, our helplessness will show them that we trust them and they will be straightforward with us and trust us as well. This can likewise mean saying 'sorry' when we misunderstand something as opposed to accusing another person. "I failed to understand the situation. What I ought to have done is…What I ought to have said is…".

Whenever you feel a child is disrespectful

Be calm and don't blow up when you think your child is being disrespectful. Distinguish the cause for disrespect and spotlight on showing problem-solving alternative.

CHAPTER THREE[1]:

DISCIPLINE

KINDNESS

The expression "discipline" originates from the Latin word "disciplinare," which means "to educate." Many individuals, be that as it may, relate the word with punishment, which misses the mark as regards the full meaning of the word. Discipline, appropriately applied, utilizes a multifaceted methodology, including modeling, rewards, and punishments that instruct and strengthen desirable conduct. Through discipline, children can learn self-control, self-awareness, capability, and a feeling of caring.

Child discipline is the methods used to forestall undesirable conduct in children. The word discipline is characterized as conferring knowledge and skill, which is aimed, at the end of the day, to instruct. Discipline is utilized by parents to show their children good desires, rules and standards. Child discipline can include rewards and punishments to show self-control, increasing desirable practices and reduction in wrong practices.

While the reason for child discipline is to create and build attractive social propensities in children, a definitive goal is to cultivate sound judgment and ethics so the child creates and keeps up self-discipline all through the remainder of his/her life. In its most broad sense, discipline alludes to orderly guidance given to a subordinate. To

---
[1]

discipline means to educate an individual to follow a specific set of accepted rules.

The word discipline intends to confer knowledge and skill – to educate. In any case, it is regularly likened with punishment and control. There is a lot of debate about the suitable approaches to discipline children, and parents are regularly befuddled about viable approaches as far as possible to impart self-control in their child.

Discipline is the structure that enables the child to fit into this present reality joyfully and adequately. It is the establishment for the improvement of the child's own self-discipline. Effective and positive discipline is tied in with educating and directing children, not simply compelling them to comply. Likewise with every single other mediation planned for calling attention to unsatisfactory conduct, the child ought to consistently realize that the parent adores and bolsters the person in question. Trust among parent and child ought to be kept up and continually.Child rearing is the assignment of bringing up children and furnishing them with the vital material and passionate consideration to advance their physical, enthusiastic, subjective and social improvement. Teaching children is one of the most significant yet troublesome duties of child rearing, and there are no alternate ways.

The rushed pace of the present society can be a snag to successful discipline. The goal of viable discipline is to encourage worthy and fitting conduct in the child and to raise well-developed grown-ups. A disciplined individual can experience happiness, is thoughtful of the needs of others, is decisive without being forceful or antagonistic, and can endure uneasiness when necessary.

The foundation of viable discipline is respect. The child ought to have the desire to regard the parent's power and furthermore the privileges of others. Irregularity in applying discipline won't help a child regard their parents. Unforgiving discipline, for example, embarrassment (boisterous attack, yelling, ridiculing) will likewise make it difficult for the child to regard and trust the parent. Hence, compelling discipline implies discipline applied with shared regard in a firm, reasonable, sensible and steady way. The goal is to shield the child from peril, help the child learn self-discipline, and build up a solid heart and an inward awareness of other's expectations and control. It ought to likewise impart values.

The American Academy of Pediatrics proposes that a successful discipline framework must contain three components. On the off chance that these three angles are on the whole present in a program of discipline, the outcome by and large is improved child conduct. The components are:

- a learning situation described by positive, steady parent-child connections
- a proactive procedure for precise educating and reinforcing of wanted practices
- a responsive technique for diminishing or killing undesired practices

There are a few reasons why children may not act appropriately, including an absence of viable disciplinary measures. Children also normally get out of hand when they are denied of adult consideration or when they are drained, exhausted, or hungry. Children from families influenced by separation and partition, poverty, substance misuse, and parental unhappiness appear to be at more serious hazard for behavioral issues. There may likewise be biologic factors, for example, consideration deficiency/hyperactivity disorders and certain dispositions that incline specific children towards trouble making. There is alsoresearch proposing that cruel disciplinary measures may really expand poor conduct.

In a perfect world, discipline depends on proper desires for every child. It ought to be utilized to set sensible cutoff points in a steady way while as yet permitting some independence. Discipline shows both social and good principles and ought to shield children from hurt by encouraging what is desirable. It ought to likewise direct children to regard the rights and needs of others.

PARENTING STYLES

Based on how they perceive and implement discipline, parents or parenting styles can generally be grouped into four, namely: Authoritarian; Authoritative; Permissive and Uninvolved. All four are described below:

AUTHORITARIAN

Authoritarian parents are regularly thought of as disciplinarians.

- They utilize a severe discipline style with little consideration. Punishment is normal.

- Communication is generally one way: from parent to child. Rules as a rule are not clarified.

- Parents with this style are ordinarily less supporting.

- Expectations are high with constrained adaptability.

Do any of thefollowing statements sound like you?

- You accept children ought to be seen and not heard.

- With regards to rules, you trust it's "my way or no way."

- You don't mull over your child's emotions.

In the event that any of those sound like you, you may be a authoritarian parent. Tyrant parents accept children ought to adhere to the standards no matter what.

Authoritarian parents are acclaimed for saying, "Since I said as much," when a child addresses the reasons for a rule. They are not keen on consideration and their emphasis is on acquiescence and obedience.

They likewise don't permit children to engage in critical thinking difficulties or situations. Rather, they make the principles and implement the results with little respect for a child's feelings.

Authoritarian parents may utilize punishments rather than discipline. So as opposed to show a child how to settle on better decisions, they put efforts into making kids feel frustrated about their errors.

Children of tyrant parents are at a higher danger of creating self-regard issues on the grounds that their sentiments aren't esteemed. They may likewise get hostile or aggressive. As opposed to improving in future, they frequently dwell on the displeasure they feel toward their parents. Since tyrant parents are frequently severe, their children may develop to turn out to be acceptable liars with an end goal to keep away from punishment.

An authoritarian parent has clear desires and outcomes, yet shows little warmth toward their child. The parent may make statements like, "since I'm your Mum, that is the reason." This is a less effective type of child rearing, and not really recommended.

AUTHORITATIVE

Authoritative parents are reasonable and nurturing, and set high, clear expectations. Children with parents who show this style will in general act naturally disciplined and have an independent mind. This style is believed to be generally gainful to children. Disciplinary principles are clear and the reasons for them are clarified. Communication is regular and suitable to the child's degree of comprehension. Authoritative parents are nurturing. Expectations and goals are high however expressed plainly. Children may have contribution to goals.

Do any of these statements sound like you?

- You put a ton of exertion into making and keeping up a positive relationship with your child.

- You clarify the reasons for your principles.

- You authorize rules and give results, yet think about your child's emotions.

On the off chance that those statements sound reflective of you, you might be an authoritative parent. Authoritative parents have rules and they use outcomes, however they also consider their children's feelings. They approve their children's sentiments, while likewise clarifying that the adults end up at last in control.

Authoritative parents put time and energy into preventing behavioral issues before they start. They also utilize positive discipline procedures to strengthen great conduct, like commendation and reward loops.

Specialists have discovered children who have authoritative parents are well on the way to become dependable grown-ups who feel good communicating their inner minds. Children raised with authoritative discipline will in general be upbeat and fruitful. They're also bound to be acceptable at settling on choices and assessing dangers all alone.

PERMISSIVE

Permissive or Indulgent parents generally let their children do what they need, and offer constrained direction or counsel. They are more like companions than parents. Their discipline style is something contrary to severe. They have restricted or no principles and generally let children make sense of issues all alone. Communication is open yet these parents let children choose for themselves instead of providing guidance. Parents tend to be warm and nurturing. Goals are normally insignificant or are not set by these parents.

Do any of these statements sound like you?

- You set principles however once in a while implement them.

- You don't give out results all the time.

- You figure your child will learn the best with little interference from you.

In the event that those statements pertain to you, you may be a permissive parent. Permissive parents are merciful. They frequently possibly step in when there's a difficult issue. They're very lenient and they embrace a mentality of "children will be kids." When they do utilize results, they may not make those outcomes stick. They may give benefits back if a child asks or they may permit a child to escape break early on the off chance that he vows to be acceptable.

Permissive parents normally take on even more of a companion job than a parent job. They regularly urge their children to converse with them about their issues, yet they for the most part don't invest a lot of energy into discouraging poor decisions or awful conduct.

Children who grow up with permissive parents are bound to compete scholastically. They may show progressively social conduct as they don't acknowledge authority and rules. They frequently have low self-regard and may report a great deal of misery.

They're also at a higher hazard for medical issues, like heftiness, on the grounds that permissive parents battle to constrain lousy feeding habits. They are considerably bound to have dental cavities on the grounds that permissive parents frequently don't authorize great propensities, like guaranteeing a child brushes his teeth.

A permissive parent shows heaps of friendship toward their child however gives little discipline. This is may sometimesbe a less effective type of parenting.

UNINVOLVED PARENTS

Uninvolved parents give children a great deal of opportunity and by and large avoid giving direction. A few parents may settle on a cognizant choice to parenting, others are less keen on parenting or uncertain of what to do.

Common traits include:

- No specific discipline style is used. An uninvolved parent lets a child for the most part do what he needs, likely out of an absence of information or caring.

- Communication is constrained.

- There are not many or no expectations of children.

Do any of these statements sound like you?

- You don't get some information about school or schoolwork.

- You infrequently know where your child is or who he/she is with.

- You don't invest a lot of energy with your child.

In the event that those statements sound more like you, you may be an uninvolved parent. Uninvolved parents will in general have little knowledge of what their children are doing. There will in general be hardly any principles. Children may not get a lot of direction, nurturing, and parental consideration. Uninvolved parents anticipate that children should raise themselves. They don't dedicate a lot of time or vitality into meeting children's fundamental needs.

Uninvolved parents might be careless however it's not always deliberate. A parent with psychological wellness issues or substance misuse issues, for instance, will most likely be unable to think about a child's physical or social needs consistently.

At different occasions, uninvolved parents need knowledge about children development. Also, once in a while, they're basically overpowered with different issues, like work, covering tabs, and dealing with a family. Children with uninvolved parents are likely to battle with self-regard issues. They will in general perform ineffectively in school. They also show behavioral conduct issues and are serially unhappy.

NOTE: There are no perfect or "best" parenting style. However there are some of the parenting styles above that are seemingly undesirable, notably the authoritarian (the over-strict, over-regulating) and the uninvolved (over-lax, totally hands-free) methods of parenting.

IMPORTANCE OF DISCIPLINING CHILDREN

Despite the fact that "discipline" regularly has a negative meaning, it is similarly as vital as affection, nourishment and other desirable virtues with regards to bringing up a child. We need to appreciate each moment with our children, so at times it very well may be trying to give boundaries to them.

There are many reasons why a parent might not have any desire to discipline a child. A few parents might be hesitant to discipline children since they need to abstain from having struggle or on the grounds that they would prefer not to have their child resent them. Others might be not able or reluctant to give time and vitality to the task of restraining children. Also, still, others may have unhappy recollections of being disciplined when they were children and might need to make things simpler on their own children by loosening up rules and giving them all the more free rein.

In any example, the truth of the matter is, discipline isn't tied in with making strife with your child or lashing out of frustration. Child discipline, when done accurately, isn't tied in with attempting to control your child however about telling her the best way to control her own behavior. It isn't tied in with punishing a child for doing something incorrectly yet about setting clear parameters and consequences for defying norms so he/she figures out how to discipline herself.

Obviously at of a the end of a long work day, when you and your child are both tired, it very well may be anything but difficult to be less steady with discipline. In any case, those minutes are similarly as significant in building up boundaries as what happens the remainder of the day. It's normal for a child to test you; truth be told, it's normal since that is the way children learn. Testing is fundamental for children to find out about their environment and discover what is adequate and what isn't. Children need to feel boundaries since that gives them security and wellbeing, which are the establishment for enthusiastic and psychological learning. At the point when children have a sense of security, they can coordinate their vitality into connecting with and investigating their general surroundings. On the off chance that those boundaries aren't set up, that child's vitality goes rather towards negative testing practices.

Children have an inborn need to feel ensured and the boundaries made by sufficient discipline satisfy that need by giving security and wellbeing. When testing heightens, this is a message to the adult– the child is essentially imploring you to stop him/her. It's significant for us to react, "I'm going to stop you since I love you." In homerooms, there are a wide range of children who every now and again test their boundaries. In these examples, they can't connect with class materials or construct associations with their companions, in light of the fact that rather they're in the method of continually asking "OK, what else would I be able to do, until somebody stops me?"

So, discipline is tied in with showing children an arrangement of qualities that they can use to control them through life. This framework can prompt a more advantageous passionate life that advances the improvement of self-inspiration, self-control, character, and dynamism. At the end of the day, discipline permits children to create self-discipline, and encourages them become genuinely and socially develop grown-ups.

Children are for the most part gas and no brakes since they don't consider results normally. You must make your child consider results. Have an easygoing discussion about how to treat individuals well, instruct them that you can't reprimand others for their decisions. Discipline tells them that you don't endure that conduct and there will be consequences for such behavior.

REASONS PARENTS NEED TO DISCIPLINE THEIR CHILDREN

There are actually a number of surprising reasons why parents need to discipline their children. They are outlined below:

Discipline Helps Kids Manage Anxiety

In all honesty, kids would prefer not to be in control. They frequently test boundaries just to ensure that their parental figures can protect them. At the point when grown-ups offer positive and negative consequences, kids develop and learn.

Children who have excessively permissive parents frequently experience tension since they need to makeadultchoices. The absence of direction and the nonattendance of authority can be very agitating for kids.

Discipline Teaches Kids to Make Good Choices

Proper discipline teaches kids how to use sound judgment. For instance, when a child loses his bike when riding into the street, he figures out how to settle on more secure choices next time.

Sound discipline teaches kids elective approaches to get their needs met. Children need to learn critical thinking skills, drive control, and self-guideline skills from proper discipline.

It is essential to recognize the distinction between consequences and punishments. At the point when children are disciplined with proper consequences they learn from their missteps. Punishments, in any case, will in general imply that kids rapidly figure out how to not get caught when they get into trouble.

Discipline Teaches Kids to Manage Emotions

At the point when a child gets a reprimand after hitting his sibling, he learns skills that will assist him with dealing with his annoyance better later on. The goal of the reprimand ought to be to teach your child to put himself in break or step away from the circumstance when he's getting upset before he gets into trouble.

Other discipline techniques, for example, encouragement, can also teach kids how to manage emotions. At the point when you state, "You are striving to assemble that tower despite the fact that it is extremely difficult to do. Keep doing awesome," finds out about the significance of enduring disappointment.

Disregarding little misbehavior can teach kids socially proper approaches to manage their dissatisfaction also.

Discipline Keeps Kids Safe

A definitive goal of discipline ought to be to protect kids. This includes significant safety issues, for example, looking at the two sides before going across the street. There ought to be consequences when your child doesn't play it safe.

Discipline ought to also address other health dangers, for example, preventing obesity. In the event that you let your child eat anything she desires, they may encounter genuine health dangers. It's essential to set sound cutoff points and offer instruction to enable your child to figure out how to settle on solid choices.

Clarify the hidden purposes behind these guidelines so your child will comprehend the safety issues. Rather than saying, "Quit hopping," when your child is bouncing on the bed, disclose to them why it's an issue. State, "You could fall and hit your head." Let them know the reason.

At the point when your child finds out about the reasons behind your rules, and he comprehends the particular safety dangers, they will be bound to consider the safety dangers when you're not there to guide them.

THE RIGHT WAY TO DISCIPLINE

Ways parents implement discipline differs from parent to parent and from culture; however some general tips might suffice:

Remain Calm

You might be enticed to let your bubbling feelings bamboozle you, however outrage and hostility won't get the message across to children; rather they will get frightened and befuddled. Attempt to take a look at an objective view or even compose a pre-created plan on acceptable behavior in a circumstance where you kid misbehaves.

Compromise and discretionally pick what you discipline

Studies show that the most impact types of discipline incorporate contribution compromises, paying little heed to the kid's degree of bad conduct.

Compromise assists kids with learning communication and urges them to look out for better conduct. Be that as it may, be warned that an excess of compromise over the long term can cause rebellious or fierce children to get into trouble all the more much of the time. Each and every issue shouldn't be a war. On the off chance that you are continually inconsistent with your kid, they will in the end block you out. Pick admirably which issues are sufficiently significant to handle.

Use reasoning

For less extraordinary practices, for example, crying or complaining, reasoning has also been demonstrated to be an impact approach to impress discipline.

In spite of the fact that it may not be as powerful at the time for particular sorts of mischief, reasoning is really the best discipline procedure in the long term.

Children can best change their behavior when they really understand why what they did wasn't right. Studies show that children are well on the way to show empathic concerns on the off chance that they have parents who assist them with managing negative feelings, so it's dependent upon you to help converse with them about how emotions influence behavior, and the other way around.

Set Limits and Stick to Them

With the hecticness that plagues families today, it very well may be hard to be consistent in your every day plans. Be that as it may, actually, kids flourish when they have structure and know their limits. At the point when the desires are unmistakably conveyed ahead of time, kids have a structure to work with.

This doesn't mean you have to go over the edge with several rules, yet center around what's generally significant for your family. Be clear about the guidelines and what happens when somebody disrupts the norms – ensure that everybody comprehends the results early and that the discipline is identified with that particular conduct.

In the event that he refuses to hold fast to your technology time limits, he loses his technology benefits for the following day or week (contingent upon the age). Yet, making her clean the carport because she didn't get her work done isn't connected and is hence not a fitting result.

Most importantly, be consistent. Finish each time with the agreed-upon result when children push the rules. However, beware so you don't become over-predictable.

Withdraw Privileges

Although a beating stings for a moment or two, removing a benefit harms longer.

Remove the TV, computer games, his preferred toy or an enjoyable activity for the afternoon and he'll have a remebrance not to rehash that botch.

Clarify when the benefits can be earned back. Generally, 24 hours is sufficiently long to show your youngster to learn from his slip-up.So you may state, "You've lost TV for the remainder of the day however you can acquire it back tomorrow by getting your toys the first occasion when I inquire."

Each child has something precious to them. It isn't wicked for that thing to become possibly the most important factor, if necessary. Most loved squishy toys, mobile phones, gaming gadgets, and so forth would all be able to be used to your advantage. On the off chance that your warnings have failed to attract your child's attention, remove a thing for a period and let your child by and by discover that actions have consequences.

Permit Natural Consequences

Natural consequences permit children to learn from their own slip-ups. For instance, if your kid says he won't wear a coat, let him head outside and get cold—as long as it's sheltered to do as such.

Use natural consequences when you figure your youngster will learn from his own misstep. Screen the circumstance to guarantee that your youngster won't experience any genuine peril.

There is a school assignment your youngster has procrastinated doing for about fourteen days. It is the prior night it is expected to be submitted and she is in a frenzy. You warned her seven days ago not to hold up until the last minute, however it happened at any rate. She is currently pleading for you to help her. Try not to support her and let her experience the aftereffect of her activities. The tension, loss of rest, and terrible evaluation will instruct her to settle on better choices next time.

Teach New Skills

As you consider how to discipline your youngster, it's essential to recall the root importance of the word, discipline – educate, teach, direct, illuminate. The most ideal approach to discipline your kid is to assist her with settling on better decisions by showing her the right behavior or reaction. Role-playing or modeling is an excellent way to do this.

For example, if your kid is experiencing problemrelating with others and this results in her hitting another child, rather than whisking her away, diffuse the tension and demonstrate her the suitable method to react.

Also, here's the fun part – switch roles and imagine you're the kid and let your little one direct you through settling on better decisions.. Try not to anticipate that your child should react fittingly after one round of role-playing. Yet, practice gains ground and progress makes more harmony in your home.

In conclusion, be encouraging when your children make the correct decisions – or even show any development in the correct way. "I see you endeavored to tidy up the kitchen completely all alone! That is such a major improvement. I truly value it." or "Thank you for offering the book to your sibling. How kind!"

One of the principal issues with spanking is that it doesn't show your kid how to act better. Spanking your child because he lost his temper, won't show him how to calm himself down whenever he's upset.

Children gain by figuring out how to tackle issues, deal with their feelings and compromise. At the point when parents encourage these skills it can incredibly decrease behavioral problems. Use discipline that is planned for instructing, not punishing.

Call a time-out.

A time-out can be particularly useful when a particular guideline is broken. This discipline instrument works best by warning children they will get a time out in the event that they don't quit, reminding them what they fouled up in as few words—and with as meager emotion—as conceivable, and expelling them from the circumstance for a pre-set period of time (1 moment for a matured kid is a decent dependable guideline). With children who are of 3 years of age, you can have a go at letting the children lead their own time-out as opposed to setting a timer. You can simply say, "Go to time out and return when you feel prepared and in charge." This procedure, which can enable the child to learn and rehearse self-administration skills, likewise functions admirably for more matured children and teens.

Commend and Reward Good Behavior

By far one of the most effective strategies for effecting quality discipline. Rather than beating a child for misbehavior, reward him for good behavior. For instance, if your kid battles with his kin frequently, set up a reward framework to inspire him to coexist better with them. Giving a motivating force to act can reduce misbehavior fast. Rewards help children to concentrate on what they have to do to win benefits, instead of underline the terrible behavior they should maintain a strategic distance from.

Prevent behavior issues by finding your childacceptable. For instance, when he's playing pleasantly with his kin, call attention to it. Say, "You are doing such a great job sharing and relating today."

When there are a few children in the room, give the most consideration and acclaim to the children who are keeping the rules and carrying on well. At that point, when the other youngster starts to act, give him commendation and consideration also.

Lead By Example

Children admire their parents, so on the off chance that you need your ability to be caring, empathetic, and understanding, you ought to be as well. You can see that when your child is youthful and learning, they absorb things like voices, mimicking sounds and behaviors, so why not give them great characteristics to mimic?

In the event that you happen to commit an error, that is alright; simply be informative with your child, so they can learn from it too.

AGE-BASED STRATEGY

While the above are somewhat generic guides as to how to go about effecting discipline with kids, there are still some specific tips that pertain to and belong to only a certain age-group of children,; and this is quite logical. Discipline strategies need to change as a child ages. What worked for your child at age 2 may not be viable at age 7.

You have to perceive when your discipline techniques are never again viable and need alteration.

Understanding that age assumes a role in the sort of discipline that is best is important. You cannot expect to employ the discipline of a toddler on a teen or adolescent who is on the way to becoming an adult. Here I will provide a division of parenting strategy based on the grouping of certain age categories:

BABIES

Babies for the most part needn't bother with discipline. They are simply finding out about the world and they don't have a grip on great versus awful behavior. That will come soon enough when they are little children.

Be that as it may, this doesn't imply that babies don't do things that require consequences. For example, we don't need our multi month old slithering over to aelectricswitch and placing their finger in it.

The key is to make a sheltered situation with the goal that the infant can investigate their reality in a protected way. On the off chance that they create behaviors, for example, hitting or contacting things they shouldn't, they can be redirected.

Redirect babies' attention. Give them something safe to contact and play with. Showing them the distinction between "yes contact" and "no touch" is fundamental. On the off chance that they can't comply with the "no touch" for a particular thing, for example, pulling the feline's hair, at that point expel the thing from their view and capacity to contact it. A few months old isn't probably going to comprehend the idea of a time out.

The key with babies is that they need love, solace, and redirection instead of discipline, for example, time outs. They are simply building up their feeling of self and finding their general surroundings. Before long enough they will be little children and consequences can turn out to be part of the routine. Up to that point, it's the parents' business to get infant far from perilous circumstances and things.

The parent can divert or redirect their child when behavior should be changed. Find innovative approaches to divert your child's attention. They needn't bother with discipline for getting the TV remote control. Rather the parent essentially needs to supplant the remote with a toy and cause the toy to show up undeniably more intriguing and fascinating than a boring remote control.

TODDLERS

Redirection of behavior is likewise useful for toddlers. You will end up saying "no-no" more than once when you have a toddler. You need to choose which behaviors are venturing over the line and require consequences. Others beahviors can essentially be redirected a lot of like you would do with them in the infant stage.

Straightforward verbal redresses are useful at this stage. At the point when the verbal redresses come up short, at that point you have to make a move. Sometimes toddlers are simply trying things out to perceive what they can pull off.

Know your cutoff points, so you sense when the behavior has gone too far and verbal recbuff just isn't sufficient. That way you can move onto different strategies, for example, time outs, removing toys, or expelling benefits (straightforward things for toddlers like no frozen yogurt).

Toddler dissolve downs and fits are the standard. In the event that you have a child who doesn't experience a hissy fit stage that includes shouting and hitting, at that point you are fortunate and your child is a unicorn. For all of us, we need a gigantic portion of persistence, profound breathing, and a calmness of our psyche and feelings when the hissy fits start.

The following tips can help better with toddlers:

- **Avoid triggers that can cause rancor**

    Attempt to stay away from triggers that may cause the fits to happen (like skirting their naptime or overlooking their tidbits and you end up with a "angry toddler"). At the point when you are out in the open, expel yourself from the open circumstance.

- **The best consequences for fits of toddlers areimposed silent times.**

    This is not the same as a time out. The time out is generally indistinguishable number of minutes from that of the child's age (on the off chance that the child is 3, at that point they get a brief time out). Fits of rage require extra time for the child to calm themselves and recoup.

- **The key with toddlers is to resist the urge to panic.**

    You should be their stone, not the one losing it when they lose it. Be clear and firm with your child. They need to see that you're in charge and that someone is in control. Keep your middle and be exceptionally firm. You can say, "We are not remaining here. We can return when you can get a hold of yourself. We are leaving now."

- **Time outs can start during the toddler stage.**

  A unique seat assigned as the time out seat is useful for making this result strategy consistent and reasonable for the toddler. You can use a timer that is assigned as the "time out" timer.

  A general rule for time out length is that the quantity of long periods of the child's age is a similar measure of minutes for the time out (for example 2 minutes for a 2-year old, 3 minutes for a 3-year old, and so forth.). In the event that the child keeps finding a workable pace timeout seat, at that point the parent needs to hold returning the child to their time out seat until their time out is finished.

- **There are a few children that do well with a time out when they can sit with Mom or Dad.**

  They need their parent there as it is a consolation that they are as yet cherished despite the fact that they are being disciplined. That works also as long as they are being expelled from their playtime and toys, the outcome of time out in their seat with Mom or Dad close to them is fine.

PRE-SCHOOLERS (2-3 YEARS)

Time outs are likewise useful for preschool matured children. The preschool age is the point at which you can start to see that some discipline strategies work for one child however they may not work for another.

In the event that you child is fixated on their fire motor truck that they need to take to the store, to chapel, and to preschool, you at that point realize it will be powerful in removing this toy for disciplinary measure if necessary. For our children it relies upon the seriousness of the activity. For hitting that caused injury to a kin they will lose that toy for a whole day.

You don't need the child to ever feel vanquished, so don't take steps to discard it because that is very harsh. Rather a time out for that toy for an assigned measure of time is suitable.

One recommended disciplinary tip that is peculiar to this age-group (but almost not practiced anywhere) is thorough reason and discussion of their behaviors.

It is significant at this stage to be increasingly thorough on reason and discussion of the behavior and consequences. You need your children to comprehend why you are removing their preferred toy or giving them a time out. You likewise need them to feel a feeling of developing good and bad in their heart and psyche.

At the point when they comprehend that their ridiculing or hitting their kin brings about hurt sentiments and physical hurt, they can start to feel for their kin torment and hurt. They will feel awful for their activities.

Possibly but not immediately, however as they develop and you are consistent with both the consequences and the calm, empathetic discussions about their activities and the subsequent consequences, you will find that they will build up a more noteworthy feeling of regret and emmpathy.

The objective isn't to just change their behavior. It is to change their heart and inspirations. You need your children to want to coexist with others and to submit to the rules. They will when they comprehend the reasons behind those rules, the clear consequences, and their feelings are engaged with the procedure.

Discipline is directing their hearts as much as it is managing their activities.

SCHOOL-AGE CHILDREN

At the point when children arrive at school age, at that point usually the period of when time outs stop. Be that as it may, there are times when calm time in their room is required. For mentality modifications and emotional episodes, room time for the child to calm themselves away from others (and hardware) is frequently useful. Some discipline hacks that are somewhat peculiar to this group, and will actually help their educational and career development include:

- **Taking away screen time**

This is where gadgets are getting increasingly significant. Regardless of whether it is an individual tablet, PDA, or TV, school age children are progressively increasingly connected to these things. It turns into a simple hotspot for viable discipline. They lose time on their electronic gadget as a ramification for rules being broken.

No child authority still can't seem to state that denying a child of screen time will be hurtful to them. On the off chance that anything simply the opposite has been demonstrated. Thusly removing screen time as a result of their behaviors can be advantageous to them in a larger number of ways than one.

Be certain the time outline is reasonable with the seriousness of the behavior. In the event that they didn't make their bed that morning, possibly an hour limitation is fine. For deliberately harming their kin property or hurting another child, the gadget can be confined for an entire day or more, contingent upon the seriousness of their behavior.

Once more, it is of most extreme significance for the child to comprehend the "why" of the rules, so they comprehend why consequences are vital when rules are broken.

- **Curbing and reducing privileges**

    This is likewise effective for school aged children. Understand your child and their wants to make this effective. For example, you may have a child that likes to go ride their bicycle around with neighborhood kids after school. They may experience gotten in problem at school for something that you esteemed deserving of confining their after school bicycle riding for a day or two. Ensure that your child understands why they are being managed the result and attempt to make the time beneficial, for example, composing an expression of remorse to the instructor or child they insulted at school.

    School age is when companions become progressively increasingly essential to kids. Socialization is a significant part of improvement. Be that as it may, when misbehavior is sufficiently extreme, at that point time with companions can be confined. "Establishing" is the thing that my parents called it. At the point when children are of youthful school age, it very well may be basically not permitting them to go to an up and coming companion's birthday party. Once more, ensure that your discipline isn't excessively harsh. In the event that they trust you are excessively harsh and serious in your disciplines, at that point feelings of disdain will frame.

    Talk with your school aged children about what disciplines they esteem reasonable or unreasonable and for what infringement specifically. Having these open discussions can assist you with growing reasonable discipline strategies that are also effective for your particular child.

DISADVANTAGES OF PUNITIVE DISCIPLINARY MEASURES

So far in this book, I have made it clear that no disciplary method is the "very best"; however it has been made clear that some exist that just do not make sense at all, especially when considering modern-day realities. Some of the negative effects of applying the wrong forms of discipline on children include the following. A good number of them are backed by research:

Psychological and brain changes

Physical harm accomplishes more than put a child in danger for things like broken bones and cuts, despite the fact that these are surely noteworthy issues. Beating also lessens mind matter and causes decreases in IQ, as per Harvard Medical School therapist Akemi Tomodo in an investigation of 1,455 people distributed as, *Reduced Prefrontal Cortical Gray Matter Volume in Young Adults Exposed to Harsh Corporal Punishment* in Neuroimage in 2010. Almost certainly, the dread and torment experienced by children causes the pressure reaction to increment. This modifies mental health when the vitality is placed into being on alert for threat as opposed to learning.

Reduced verbal prowess and communication problems

Children who are spanked regularly as a type of discipline have less verbal capacity at age 5 then their counterparts who are not spanked. They likewise show all the more externalizing behaviors, for example, animosity, as indicated by Columbia University educator Michael MacKenzie and his associates in an investigation of 4,200 children distributed as "Beating and Child Behavioral and Cognitive Outcomes Through 5 Years old enough" in Infant and Child Development in 2014. The individuals who are hit will in general have less capacity to perceive sounds and more problem talking than the individuals who are not physically punished, which may influence the two scholastics and social working. Scientists empower a stage away from belts and smacks and toward different other options, which may incorporate open conversation or "time ins" where parents sit with their children until they calm down and can be addressed calmly.

Anxiety and poor social development

Physical discipline leads to anxiety and aggression. These behaviors can influence children at school and may push them into problem or cause other children to stay away from them, leading to social issues. In any event, when maternal warmth — like snuggling or other help behaviors — is high, these impacts despite everything happen because of physical discipline. Grasping maternal warmth and backing without the physical discipline might be progressively effective in expanding association and furnishing children with a base for needing to satisfy the parent. This may lessen undesirable behaviors and lead to less anxiety and aggression overall.

Bad Discipline is no Discipline

In addition to the fact that hitting increases negative behaviors like aggression, however any measure of spanking is ineffective overall. While a few children stop a behavior in the present moment after a spanking, they are bound to keep on doing it in the long haul, particularly when parents are nowhere to be found. Utilizing discipline strategies that clarify all the more briefly why these behaviors aren't right on a level other than, "Because you'll get injured on the off chance that you do it," is fundamental to halting behaviors in the long haul and lessening negative behaviors that expansion with hitting.

RETHINKING DISCIPLINE

Discipline is not supposed to be a bad word; the Latin word for it means the same as to teaching or instruction. I think that is why we refer to a person's discipline as his career. As such our actions in effecting discipline with our children should reflect this notion. We need a paradigm shift in thinking discipline from seeing it as a word that reeks corporal punishment to a word that incorporates the entire developmental process of our kids; we must spanking thse kids and start teaching them.

CHAPTER FOUR:

ROLE MODELING

COLLABORATION

So far we have talked about Independence, Trust and Respect as well as proper Discipline. All thse have to deal with the parents relationship with the child and do not place any focus on the parents themselves. Parents themselves need to work on themselves. Someone who will build another successful person must be a successful person as well, at least, on the inside. So in discussing parents as reole models, we will place some emphasis on the role of personal and cognitive development of parents, before we examine the broader concept of role modeling.

Role models are frequently subjects of profound respect and copying. Through their own characteristics and accomplishments, they can motivate others to endeavor and create without direct guidance. Because of their ordinary nearness and collaboration with their children.

Parents can fill in as consistent and advancing role models for their children. parents can be role models for learning by incorporating what school-age children have just learned into every day life.

Children are conceived without social information or social skills, and they energetically search for somebody to mimic. That "somebody" is normally one or the two parents. Parents are a child's first instructors and role models. Furthermore, for the most part children are more influenced by what their parents do than by what their parents state. They figure out how to carry on by perceiving how their moms and fathers act and by following their example.

Utilizing social skills is an incredible method to model positive behavior and lift a child's fearlessness. A child learns great habits all the more effectively when "please" and "thank you" are a part of everyday life.

Show regard for other people. Parents who regularly put down others are showing their children that others are not significant. On the off chance that you need your child to regard others, at that point regard your child. Urge all relatives to approach each other with deference.

Being consistent in educating and setting examples is significant. In the event that you tell your child that he should not hit individuals and, at that point give him a spanking as discipline for his misbehavior, your child will get confused by the blended signs.

Parents aren't perfect. We lose our tempers, make statements we are upset for and are not generally as kind as we might want to be. We are human. It is critical to concede our mistakes, state we're grieved, and show that we attempt to make things right. Being a positive role model for your children is one of the most significant and rewarding things you can accomplish for your child. As a parent,

Role models are regularly subjects of reverence and imitating. Through their own characteristics and accomplishments, they can motivate others to endeavor and create without direct guidance. Because of their standard nearness and communication with their children, parents can fill in as consistent and developing role models for their children. parents can be role models for learning by incorporating what school-age children have just learned into day by day life.

Parents aren't perfect. We lose our tempers, make statements we are upset for and are not generally as kind as we might want to be. We are human. It is important to concede our mistakes, state we're grieved, and show that we attempt to make things right. Being a positive role model for your children is one of the most significant and rewarding things you can accomplish for your child.

Role models are frequently subjects of deference and copying. Through their own characteristics and accomplishments, they can move others to endeavor and create without direct guidance. Because of their ordinary nearness and connection with their children, Parents can fill in as consistent and developing role models for their children. parents can be role models for learning by coordinating what school-age children have just learned into day by day life.

Children are conceived without social information or social skills, and they anxiously search for somebody to impersonate. That "somebody" is typically one or the two parents. Parents are a child's first instructors and role models. Furthermore, as a rule children are more influenced by what their parents do than by what their parents state. They figure out how to act by perceiving how their moms and fathers carry on and by following their example.

Utilizing social skills is an extraordinary method to model positive behavior and lift a child's self-assurance. A child learns great habits all the more effectively when "please" and "thank you" are a part of day by day life.

Show regard for other people. Parents who regularly put down others are showing their children that others are not significant. On the off chance that you need your child to regard others, at that point regard your child. Urge all relatives to approach each other with deference.

Being consistent in instructing and setting examples is significant. In the event that you tell your child that he should not hit individuals and, at that point give him a spanking as discipline for his misbehavior, your child will get confused by the blended signs.

Parents aren't perfect. We lose our tempers, make statements we are upset for and are not generally as kind as we might want to be. We are human. It is important to concede our mistakes, state we're grieved, and show that we attempt to make things right. Being a positive role model for your children is one of the most significant and rewarding things you can accomplish for your child.

As a parent, What you do shows your child how you need her to act. For example, how you adapt to sentiments like disappointment and misery impacts how your child manages her feelings. What you eat, the amount you exercise, and what you look like after yourself all impact your child.

What you state is also significant. You can assist your child with managing and control his behavior by discussing how behavior influences others. You can likewise talk more with your child about the contrasts among good and bad. Presently's a decent time for this because your child is building up his capacity to understand others' experiences and sentiments.

How you carry on imparts a sign to your child this is the kind of behavior you endorse of. In the event that what children see from your behavior is not quite the same as what they are being told, at that point your child is probably going to get confused, and potentially angry. It might likewise obscure desires and limits, leading to struggle and disappointment among you and your child.

Role modeling works corresponding to for all intents and purposes everything – from how you handle feelings, for example, dissatisfaction and outrage, to how you regard and identify with others, to how you react to pressure and adapt to troubles. It likewise impacts examples, for example, eating, work out, what you look like after yourself, and critical thinking.

HOW CAN YOU BE AN EXCELLENT ROLE MODEL FOR YOUR CHILD?

Walk the Talk

Unfortunately for parents, the idiom "Do as I state, not as I do" basically doesn't work. Children can track down hypocrisy like a dog, and they learn the most from parents who exhibit consistency between their activities and their qualities by "walking the talk."

On the off chance that you don't need your children to mislead escape going to school by pretending ailment, at that point you best not lie about taking a "wiped out" day from work.

On the off chance that you don't need your children to invest unnecessary energy in technology gadgets, you need to confine your use of similar gadgets.

Children regard grown-ups who live by the rules they lecture. Hypocrisy frustrates children and sends them searching for elective role models to follow.

Be a Model through what you say

Your children are not just watching you cautiously for signs about how to be; they are also tuning in to you. The manner in which you talk, what you talk about, and the sentiments you express will impact their qualities.

Consider how you address them, your spouse, your friends and neighbors, the registration individual at the supermarket.

Do you model respect of others through your words and manner of speaking?

Do your words show respect for differences and resilience toward all individuals or do they subtly bolster absence of acknowledgment for others unique in relation to yourself?

Do you "bully" your children with harsh words and dangers when they act up, or do you react with discipline dependent on respect for your children's humanity?

Forge Close Rapport with your kids

You will be a bigger impact in your children's lives on the off chance that you have a warm and sustaining relationship with them, and your children are bound to copy you in the event that they feel near you and bolstered by you.

Give them genuine love in a protected domain that likewise gives consistent, firm, and flexible discipline so they comprehend what is anticipated from them.

Hear them out without judgment when they are upset. Offer your own emotions with them so they find a good pace; share a portion of your decisions and dynamic as examples to control them.

Discover approaches to play around with them, to share interests, to appreciate each other's conversation (setting up a supper, talking about a TV appear, playing sports together, and so on.).

Build an association with them dependent on trust so they realize they can rely on you when they need you, thus that they figure out how to be reliable consequently.

Be a Good Role Model through your actions

Your children will see you living these lessons in the event that you are benevolent to yourself when you commit an error and in the event that you are tolerating of them when they do. Furthermore, in the event that you address issues and clashes in your own life, (for example, attempting to shed pounds or managing a troublesome neighbor) and offer the procedure with your children during a time suitable way, you can urge your children to address their interests comparatively.

You are modeling for your children a way to deal with life that remembers for going development, learning, improvement, and advancement. What an incredible life lesson for your children to learn.

It takes such a great amount of weight off them (they don't need to be perfect) because you have modeled for them how to treat themselves as well as other people when the unavoidable wreckage ups occur. What a cheerful and idealistic demeanor to give to your children!

Be the version of yourself that you want your children to be

Ask yourself what kind from individuals you need your children to become, and afterward consider what you can do to model the behaviors and mentalities that would mirror that kind of individual. This is another method for saying that it is useful for you to inspect your own qualities.

For example, do you need your children to:

- build up a hard working attitude?
- Be generous?
- have courage?
- go to bat for their beliefs?
- be kind and obliging?
- be diligent and industrious?
- be self-assured?
- be a contributing member of society?
- take great care of their bodies?
- be available to new learning? To discover delight in curiosity?

In the event that you wish for these qualities in your children, at that point do these things yourself!

CONCLUSION – *LOOK AFTER YOURSELF*

Being the best parent you can be and supporting your child through their high school years requires persistence, calmness, time and strength. Despite the fact that your family is a need, they also depend on you. Make your own wellbeing as significant as that of your family, and don't feel remorseful for requiring time to yourself. Protection, space, harmony and calm are frequently expected to recharge your batteries so you can address your family's issues.

Nobody can do only it – in the event that you need support, connect with individuals you trust and respect for counsel. You may locate that different parents have comparable experiences, and it tends to be ameliorating to know you're not the only one in feeling overpowered now and again.

www.ingramcontent.com/pod-product-compliance
Lightning Source LLC
Chambersburg PA
CBHW050306120526
44590CB00016B/2506